A Spiny Back

Back

and

Green Scaly

Skin

Whose Little Baby Are You?

by Ellen Lawrence

Published in 2016 by Ruby Tuesday Books Ltd.

Editor: Mark J. Sachner
Designer: Emma Randall
Production: John Lingham
With thanks to Stephen Hammack,
Herpetarium Keeper, St. Louis Zoo

Photo Credits:
Alamy: 6–7, 11, 13, 18; Cosmographics: 23 (top);
FLPA: 7 (top), 20–21; Shutterstock: Cover, 1, 4–5,
6–7, 8–9, 10, 12–13, 15, 16–17, 19, 22, 23 (bottom);
Superstock: 14.

Library of Congress Control Number: 2015940230

ISBN 978-1-910549-22-3

Printed and published in the United States of America

For further information including rights and permissions requests, please contact our Customer Service Department at 877-337-8577.

Contents

Words shown in **bold** in the text are
explained in the glossary.

A Baby in a Forest

Forest

In a warm forest on a **tropical** island, there lives a baby animal.

The little animal spends all her time in the leafy branches of the trees.

The baby has **scaly** skin.

She is bright green—just like the leaves on the trees.

Scaly skin

Whose little baby is this?

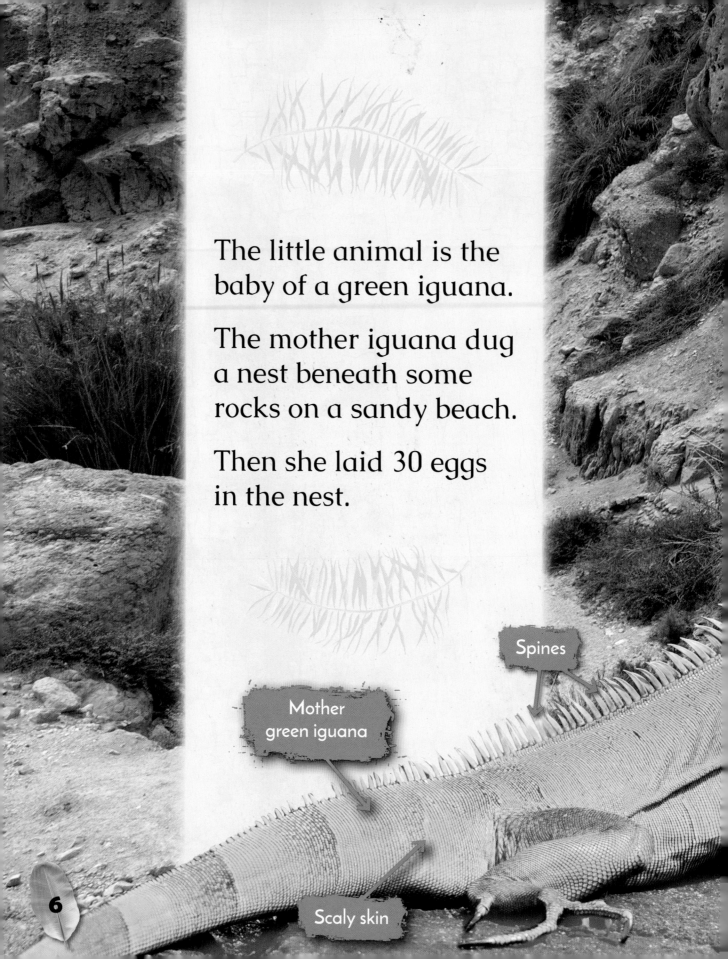

The little animal is the baby of a green iguana.

The mother iguana dug a nest beneath some rocks on a sandy beach.

Then she laid 30 eggs in the nest.

Spines

Mother green iguana

Scaly skin

Iguana eggs

The eggs have soft, leathery shells.

Nest

Once the mother iguana laid her eggs, she left the nest.

She does not take care of her eggs or babies.

Now, three months have passed by.

Egg

A tiny green iguana **hatches** from one of the eggs.

8

A baby green iguana

The baby iguana scampers out of the nest.

She quickly climbs into a tree and hides among the leaves.

Here, she is safe from snakes, large birds, and other **predators** that may try to eat her.

From her snout to the tip of her tail, the baby iguana measures 8 inches (20 cm) long.

Snout

She has long toes with sharp claws.

Toe

Tail

A one-day-old green iguana

She uses her toes and claws to hold on tight to branches.

The little iguana's brothers and sisters hatch from their eggs, too.

During their first year, the baby iguanas live close to each other.

When they are hungry, they eat leaves and flowers.

Spines

When the iguana
is about one year
old, the spines on
her back start
to grow.

By the time the iguana is two years old, she has long spines on her back.

Spines

A two-year-old iguana

Now, she is 30 inches (76 cm) long.

Not all green iguanas are green!

A three-year-old iguana

18

As the iguana grows older, her scaly skin turns grayish-green.

Some green iguanas have blue
or orange skin.

When she is four years old, the iguana is all grown up.

She spends her time resting in trees and looking for plants to eat.

One day, she will lay eggs and have babies of her own.

A four-year-old iguana

Fact File

All About Green Iguanas

One-day-old green iguanas

Green iguanas are a type of large lizard.

Both baby and adult green iguanas eat leaves and other plant foods.

If a predator bites or tears off an iguana's tail, the tail will usually grow back!

Lizards belong to an animal group known as reptiles. Reptiles have scaly skin and are **cold-blooded**. Snakes and turtles are also reptiles.

Green Iguana Size

Woman

Man

Adult green iguana

Green Iguana Weight

Adult green iguana:
Up to 20 pounds (9 kg)

Newly hatched green iguana:
3.5 ounces (100 g)

Where Do Green Iguanas Live?

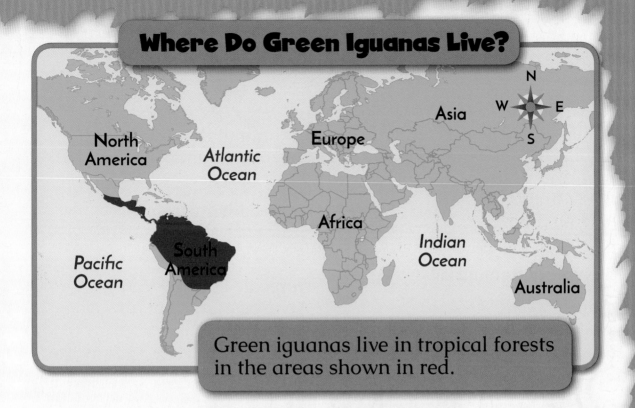

North America

Atlantic Ocean

Europe

Asia

N
W E
S

Pacific Ocean

South America

Africa

Indian Ocean

Australia

Green iguanas live in tropical forests in the areas shown in red.

Male Green Iguanas

Male iguana

An iguana has a flap of skin under its chin called a dewlap.

Dewlap

Male iguanas sometimes fight each other. They do this to decide who will get to **mate** with a female iguana.

A male iguana has a bigger dewlap than a female.

23

Glossary

cold-blooded
(kohld-BLUHD-id)
Having a body temperature
that rises or drops with
the temperature of its
surroundings.

hatches (HACH-iz)
Breaks out from inside an egg.

mate (MATE)
To get together to have babies.

predator (PRED-uh-tur)
An animal that hunts and
eats other animals.

scaly (SCAY-lee)
Covered with scales.
Scales are small sections
of overlapping skin.

tropical (TROP-i-kuhl)
An area that is hot all
year round.

Index

Read More

De la Bedoyere, Camilla.
*The Wild Life of Lizards
(The Wild Side).* New York:
Rosen Publishing (2015).

Lawrence, Ellen. *A Chameleon's
Life (Animal Diaries: Life
Cycles).* New York: Bearport
Publishing (2013).

Learn More Online

To learn more about iguanas, go to
www.rubytuesdaybooks.com/whoselittlebaby